It's A
Funny
Old Life

It's A Funny Old Life

A Collection Of Humorous Poems

J. B. EDEN

authorHOUSE®

AuthorHouse™
1663 Liberty Drive
Bloomington, IN 47403
www.authorhouse.com
Phone: 1-800-839-8640

Published by AuthorHouse   12/07/2012

ISBN: 978-1-4772-4669-6 (sc)
ISBN: 978-1-4772-4750-1 (e)

Thanks to my husband for his help and faith in me!

Contents

SPORTS TALK

THE SPORTSMAN

Golf clubs,
Fishing rod,
Tennis racquet, too.
He's really quite a sportsman;
How about you?
Can you hit a golf ball?
Can you catch a fish?
How about a game for two?
I wish!

GOLF

You can play a round of golf
All by yourself,
Or join with several friends.
The courses vary everywhere
With lots of twists and bends,
A hillock here, a woodland there
And lots of roughs, with greens to spare.
A hole in one or maybe two,
How many strokes? That's up to you!

The golfers give it all they've got.
If only they could make that shot—
The one that takes them to the top
Of the board in the bar, so near, so far!
With a hole in one comes such a thrill
Which soon wears off when presented with the bill
For the drinks all round, well, that's the deal.
Worth it, though! The dream is real.

FOOTBALL

Twenty two men running up and down
A large open space, just outside the town.
They keep falling over, I don't know why.
You'd think they'd try to keep their sporty shorts dry!
They aim to kick a ball between the goal posts
Visitors want to win and beat their hosts.
When they strike lucky they jump and hug.
This football thing is quite a bug!
You have to be keen to follow your team;
To follow the World Cup dream.
Oh no, there's the ref signalling away
Their best player, not a good day!
They really need a lot of luck to get right to the top.
As for me, well all-in-all, I think I'd rather shop!

FISHING

What is it about fishing?
It really seems a lark,
Do you know they even do it in the dark!

A stool, a rod, a tin of bait:
Then the anglers sit still and wait and wait
And wait—
Until
After several hours,
A jiggle on the line.
A slippery, slithery fish is caught.
Now all is going fine.
But
What happens next is just a pain;
They throw the poor fish back again!

WHAT NOW?

(post Olympics, 2012)

Where to go now,
How about you?
The Olympics are over, what a to-do!
Many medals were won;
It was tearful and fun.

Lots of huge smiles and running of miles,
Terrific high jumps and quite a few bumps!
Let's relish the truly sporting fact
And hope it lasts with real impact.
Yet
For some it was sad and hopes were dashed:
(And goodness me the euro crashed!)

PLACES TO GO

CAR BOOT SALE

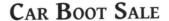

Nic-nac, bric-a-brac, car boot sale!

Early morning rush hour to the designated field.
Cars of many colours: come, see what their boots yield.
The shoppers start arriving with families in tow;
Some to rummage, some to browse, while others come
and go
Between the rows of vehicles disgorging all their wares:
The sight of Auntie Edna is causing many stares.
She has opened up her Mini boot and dragged out lots
of clothes;
Hey! That's Uncle Bert's allotment coat; I wonder if he
knows?
Amongst the piles of jumble appears a fearsome
sight—
A most dishevelled tabby cat, struggling with all her
might!
"Hell's bells!" shrieks Auntie Edna, "you'll be the death
of me:
No! Don't sit there-you're not for sale; lay underneath
that tree."
"What's that awful, yukky smell?" a childish voice is
heard.
"Its really quite er—pongy, but I can't think of the
word . . . ."
Embarrassed Mother whispers, loudly from behind,
"Its Betty Eden's pickles. Now don't be so unkind!"

The pace is getting quicker.
The crowd is getting thicker.

Only another hour to go before the bartering stops.
The sellers start to pack away their various unsold lots.
Its time to leave the battle field and join the traffic jam.
Fold up the pasting table, re-pack that unsold pram,
Perhaps we'll come again next week, its worth another
try,
And anyway, its good to meet another jumbled guy!

The field is now deserted; its grass is rather flat.
But wait a mo. What's over there?
Its Auntie Edna's cat!

THE EASTER FAIR

"Everyone a winner,
Roll up, roll up: don't barge!"
Calls out the man in charge.

Another shout from over there
A lady on a stall joins in; a member of the fair,
"Come here to me my lovely, just stand here on the right.
Come over here and try your hand, promise I won't bite!
Fish for a pretty yellow duck.
Come over here and try your luck."

We could bring home a coconut
Or a bear so soft and brown
Come on, let's go and have some fun.
The fair has come to town!

A Lot of Hot Air

A hot air balloon festival used to be held in Southampton
(sadly missed)

They are visible now, though still far away,
But coming much closer.
With the currents of air you can see them sway.

A magical sight for anyone's eyes.
Look at the colours.
Now they're right overhead,—my, what a size!

With a roar from the burner, a shout from the crew,
"We can't land here."
Now they're floating away to pastures new.

Seashore Memories

Waves roar,
Water pounds.
The shingle rattles,
So many sounds!
Sparkling droplets
And salty spray;
Seagulls land
Then fly away.

Boats at anchor
Rocking, then still.
A cormorant dives—
A fish in its bill!
A child digs deep
In soft golden sand;
Mother calls
Icecream in hand.

Seaside,
Dreamy days,
Seahorse summer,
Lazy ways.
Sudden splashes,
Tingling checks,
The smell of seaweed—
Halcyon weeks!

THE BISHOPS PUB AT ST DAVIDS

We're sitting at table fifty one
Enjoying the view and the autumn sun.
I can see the Bishop's Palace from here;
St Davids Cathedral is very near.

We're eating the local crab for tea,
With crusty bread, just right for me!
Then down to the coast, around the bay,
A lovely sunset, a lovely day.

I Wish

I hear the hooter blowing,
A cruise ship's going out.
The note is deep and haunting
As the tugs turn her about.

From ship to shore they're waving.
"Look, there's Aunty Flo,
That space near her she's saving
For Sam and Uncle Joe!"

They sail to distant sunshine
While we return to work.
Perhaps I'll ask my company
"A rise, a cruise, a perk?"

The boss will think I'm crazy
But you never know,
I might get lucky one day
And cruise like Uncle Joe!

WEATHER WORRIES

A British Winter

Coughs and colds, 'flu and sneezes;
Winter brings its own diseases.
How I hate the winter!

Frozen fingers, chilblain toes—
Winter brings a bright red nose.
How I loathe the winter!

Icy Hampshire, fog-bound Dorset;
Itchy vests and too-tight corset.
Oh, I hate the winter!

Summer?

Rain, rain, same again!
Drip,
    drop,
        patter,
            plop.
Will this deluge never stop?

Sun climb, rise and shine.
Shed light, warm and bright
Happy, brilliant, super sight!

THE WET JULY

Its true! I wouldn't lie to you.
The rain has stopped—the sky is blue.
Let's make the most of this respite,
Take a walk, fly a kite,
Kick a ball, go for a ride,
Then clear up the mess when the floods subside.

And what a mess its left for us.
We'll try not to cry or make a fuss.
Yet its difficult to see it through,
Will things be different when we do?
But the rain has stopped—the sky is blue.
We'll mop till we drop
While the sun shines through.

THE DRYING MACHINE

It moves across the sky in a wondrous arc,
Shining on the meadows
And the playground in the park.
It brings us light and happiness with benefits galore
You really are 'my sunshine',
Please shine on us some more.

I know we need the rain as well
But not to cause a flood;
We need the sun to beam right down
And dry up all the mud!

DECISIONS

The sky is bright but the clouds are grey.
What will the weather do today?

I'm going out: at the weather I stare,
I might get wet, don't usually care,
But the thing I really want to wear
Is my baby Alpaca; shall I dare?
It might get soaked; it was made in Peru.
It feels so soft and the colour is blue.

The choice is mine, a chance to take?
I'm not that brave, for goodness sake!

NOTES ON HEALTH

SLEEPLESS NIGHTS

I had a cup of tea at half past three
And now its ten past four.
I'll lie quite still and take deep breaths
Then maybe I'll fall asleep.
When I open my eyes its twenty to five—
Enough to make you weep!
OK, repose—
Now, wiggle your toes
I've heard that helps a lot.

I think I'm drifting off at last,
When daybreak shows the night is past.

Good gracious, look!
Its half past seven.
Those last two hours were heaven.

Ouch!

All went well 'til I reached sixty-five,
From that time on things began to dive!
I broke my shoulder at Hay-on-Wye
How stupid is that—but I didn't cry.
Hereford hospital helped with some pills
And a sling for support when it kills!
The pills wore off and the pain was quite bad
But I missed Jo Brand, which was really sad!

That was a taster for the next big deal.
Another twist and turn of nature's wheel.

Now its summer-time and the holiday is nigh
Cornwall beckoned with a clear blue sky.
We swam with the Grandsons, splashed and had fun,
Booked a badminton court for half past one.
With a wonderful shot came a mighty loud crack;
Achilles tendon gone and I'm on my back.
The A&E at Truro gave crutches and a plaster,
No holiday now, just another disaster!

P–M–R

Polymyalgia Rheumatica
P—M—R!
Its pain is quite fantastica
P—M—R!

It blights your life,
Brings pain and strife;
It really makes you paranoid.
But wait, there's help: its steranoid!

Oh yes, it copes,
We have great hopes.
Its just a shame, but who's to blame?
The side effects bring pain the same.
(Although in different places!)

Unwanted Feeling!

Pain, pain go away
Never to return.
I've had enough of you, you know
All you do is burn.
Sometimes crackle, sometimes spurt,
All you ever do is hurt.
Your fiery nature's hard to bear.
You prick, you stab, you tear.
Then, when I think you've done your worst
You smoulder on—
I think I'm cursed!

ARACHNOPHOBIA

Got up this morning feeling bright
Until I saw that spider.
It gave me such a fright!

I sat up on the table (it was so big and hairy)
And watched it run around: it really was quite scary.
At last it ran beneath the door.
Now I could put my feet to floor!

LAUGHTER

Laughter is lovely!
Effervescent, bubbly;
Chuckles and hiccups
And trips off the tongue.
It can be infectious,
Spreading like wildfire:
Or secret and solitary,
Not to be shared.

There's a thin line dividing
The laughter from crying,
Uncontrollable hysteria,
Streaming tears.
Both have their place
Fulfilling a need:
Crying for cleansing
And laughter promoting
The help that is coming to heal.

ALL SORTS

To those like me

(who many don't see)

To many I seem invisible, only noticed by a few.
To the rest I'm non-existent, no matter what I do!
I think I'll change my image: go punk and have pink hair,
With lots of dangly earrings, and outrageous clothes.
(Will I dare?)
Should I speak with a foreign accent?
Or develop a fancy walk?
If I wear huge hats and hot pants
Will *that* make them talk?
I suppose it's a matter of presence, and I'm sadly lacking
that.
Perhaps I should be more forceful; be loud-mouthed—
(and get really fat.)
I think I will start tomorrow.
Today I'll consider and plot.
Watch paint dry and finish my knitting,
Then go out and astonish the lot!
Not sure about the hair, though: will the pink be a bit
<u>too</u> pink?
The earrings are pretty heavy; I'll have lobes to my
waist, I should think!
And its much too cold for hot pants—my varicose veins
will freeze.

My kneecaps will simply shiver, and I'll probably start
to wheeze!
Will they notice my transformation?
Will they hear me when I speak?
Do I want this recognition? Do I want to look a freak?
Maybe I'll stay invisible: it might be useful yet.
As long as **I** remember me. (In case the rest forget!)

GUESS WHAT

We use it here,
We use it there.
We use it almost everywhere.

It doesn't smell,
Will never tell,
And always travels very well.

Look, this is mine
With a hologram sign,
A sunset and a swaying pine.

I'm sure you've guessed.
Its not so hard.
Its our friendly, flexible credit card!

NURSERY RHYME

(for business men & women!)

Hey ho,
Don't be slow;
You'll lose the race.

See saw,
Hide that flaw
Or you'll lose face!

Dear me—
Nothing's free.
Change that clause.

Tic tac,
Scratch my back
And I'll scratch your's!

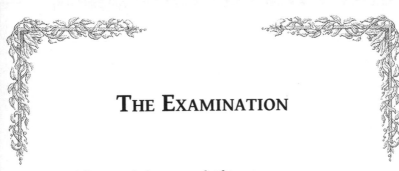

THE EXAMINATION

The candidates are drifting in
One or two,
A group, a few.
A sudden rush as time draws near
Six, seven, eight appear.

With bags and coats put at the back,
A jumbled row
A heap, to show
No-one can cheat with hidden books
Almost time—worried looks.

The invigilator reads the rules;
Glances round
All tense, no sound.
"You may begin," she says at last.
Thirty pens writing fast!

With concentration evident.
A quiet room, a cough,
Some gloom.
Scratching pens and heads bent low,
As the pace begins to show.

"Stop writing now," a voice commands.
Three hours gone by,
It seemed to fly.
Both panic and relief is shown.
Some students smile while others groan.

The candidates are filing out.
"What about that?"
They jostle and chat.
All tension gone, at least for today.
Goodbye hard work and hello play!

Too Much TV

I watch the television with one eye on the clock;
One arm in a jumper, one foot in a sock.
I'm not a watch-a-holic
But I cannot bear to go
Until I know the answer—
Will she marry Jim or Joe?
And will that woman have to do a lengthy spell in jail,
Or will her lawyers win and the prosecution fail?
I know its only make believe
But it sometimes gives me colic.
Me? No, never,
I'm not a watch-a-holic!

MODERN CHANT

Don't drool man.
Stay cool man.
We rule man.
OK?

Hey! You man.
Stay true man.
You're new man.
OK?

MOVING MOMENTS

Happy as the day is long
Trilling out a tuneless song,
She waves her duster up and down
Then pauses briefly, with a frown.
"I'm sure I didn't put it here.
Not with the daffodils so near.
That pollen, it falls everywhere
I'm sure I put it over there!"

But what it was we'll never know
Because she tripped and stubbed her toe.
And when composure was regained
She'd quite forgotten just how pained
The moving item made her feel:
This new pain in her toe was real.
It makes a tear come to her eye,
She folds her duster with a sigh.

No more tuneless songs today.
She makes her mind up right away.
"I'll go and get myself a treat
A choccy bar for me to eat."
And while she searches through the cupboard
Hums aloud 'Old Mother Hubbard'.
Then, as she munches through the bar,
Turns round and knocks the coffee jar!

"Right! That's done it. I'm going out."
She sheds her pinny with a shout.
"I've had enough of dust and dirt,
I'll go to town and buy a skirt!"

TOM TICKLE

He just loves being tickled.
When you stop he squeals for more;
Then dissolves in a fit of giggles,
A jelly blob on the floor.

He tumbles about like a bear cub
Rolling and grinning with glee.
Then builds a tall brick tower
And knocks it down with his knee!

He sits on the black and white cushion
Shaped like a sleeping cat.
He puts his arms around its neck
And gives its tail a pat.

Tom Tickle's feeling rather tired,
Its been a busy day.
He mutters baby grumbles
While we put his toys away.

The bubbly bath is ready now,
Time for splashy fun.
Then, warm and dry and ready for bed,
Life's great when you're just one!

FIVE BOYS

One boy wide awake
Sailing boats on a lake.
Another boy feeling ill
Has to lie very still!
One boy, oh so strong,
Pulls a heavy cart along.
Another boy by himself
Looks at books on the shelf.
One boy out to play
Has a very happy day!

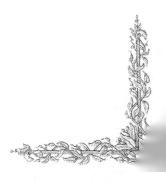

NEW BORN

Tiny, tiny fingers,
Little button nose,
Quite a lot of fluffy hair
And skin just like a rose.
Eyes so clear and baby blue,
Feet so perfectly formed.
We sighed and smiled, as adults do
When newborn suddenly yawned.

He moved, he stretched, he wriggled!
We watched and seemed amazed.
Another living miracle.
The babe just lay and gazed.

A tiny boy is lying here
Waiting for a name.
What will it be?
But one thing's sure—
He's destined, of course, for fame!

OFFICE AFFAIRS

Typewriters chatter,
Keyboards clatter,
All hands to work—
There's no time to shirk!
"We've got lots to do
And its all up to you."
The manager calls
As the paper falls
From the whirring, purring machine.

The office is busy,
They all feel dizzy.
Its time for a break
For goodness sake!
"All right, calm down,"
He says with a frown.
"We'll stop for tea,
But could two or three
Just carry on in-between?"

Finished at last!
Its already half past,
But at least that's done,
Now its time for some fun.
So the staff, full of glee,
Glad to be free
Dash into the rain
For the bus or the train:
Into the rush hour stream.

Now all is still.
Its peaceful until
The cleaners come in
To empty each bin
And vacuum the floor
And bang on the door!
They sing and shout
Before they go out,
Then, bliss—the office can dream.

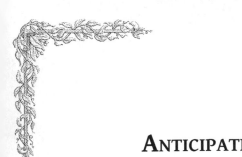

ANTICIPATION!

I think I've won the lottery,
(At least I might have done)
I'm checking numbers now
One-by-one.

Hooray that's one I've got
Its good old number three!
Now for the rest, don't hold your breath
Let me see.

Uh-oh, I haven't got that one.
I changed it just last week.
Its such a shame,
Just me to blame.
Now four to go and seek.

With great regret I have to say
I won't be waving flags today.
However, not to be deterred,
(Although a win would be preferred)
I'll have another go some time
And if I win I'll change this rhyme!

Secret Slimmer

I'm on a diet.
Quiet!

Don't tell a soul.
I want to surprise with my trim new figure,
Hopefully smaller, not bigger.

Don't snigger!

A curse on cream cakes and all the tray bakes.
Goodbye baguettes with lots of butter,
Sausage rolls, pork pies, crisps and meringues;
Then there's always the alcohol flutter!
Melt-in-mouth pastries and rich casseroles;
Oh, don't think about them—
Think health and vitality, lots of new energy;
So long as it works—
Goodbye chocolate perks
And give a big welcome to new slinky skirts!

Moving Times

We're moving today, hip, hip, hooray!
Let's hope it all goes well.

The lorry's here, don't shed a tear
The move will be just swell.

I've packed the books despite your looks:
Now for the kitchen stuff.
Hey! Where's the cat? Oh no, oh drat.
I think I've had enough.

Let's have a rest, we've done our best,
The pros can have a go.

The lorry's fit to burst
And we've worked up quite a thirst,
So goodbye empty house.

We're off to pastures new
To down a glass or two
Of last year's rhubarb wine.

Our move is going fine!

Hair Raising Talk

I despair of my hair!

It used to be thick,
It used to be brown.
But now it simply makes me frown.
Its very thin and going grey.
I can't control it, night or day.
I've tried so many preparations
No success, no celebrations.

Wait a mo—hang on a jig;
I've found the answer, get a wig!

VANITY

My arms are very hairy,
To me they look quite scary!

Its really such a trouble
'Cos shaving them leaves stubble
And that is oh so prickly;
Let's think of something quickly.

Well, long sleeved blouses come to mind.
Oh! Don't be vain and then you'll find
It doesn't matter anyway.
Problem solved—hip hooray!

THE GARDENER (1)

She filled two wheel barrows with mulch for the marrows,
Then ran down the lawn to check the sweetcorn.
There's so much to do! Will she ever get through?

All day long she dug and raked, weeded, mulched
without a break.
Two hours at the Manor and three with Mrs Tanner.
Then off to tend the grounds at the pretty Fox and
Hounds.

THE GARDENER (2)

Ouch, ouch, a crack in my back!
That's torn it for today.
"Mind how you go, use that hoe."
I hear my Mother say.
I really wish I'd listened
But I used the fork instead.
Now my back's a ruddy pain
And I'm stuck right here in bed!

DAVE'S ALLOTMENT

Watch out, there's a thief about!

I came to pick some vegetables
Walked past the shed and bale of hay
Then stopped to stare—
The ground was bare!
The rhubarb gone and lettuce, too,
And all those onions for my stew!
Who stripped my beans and petit peas?
I'd give them away for a little 'please'.
But someone couldn't be that fair
They stole and didn't leave a share.

I'll have to think quite hard its clear,
Before I dig and plant next year.

PUPPY LOVE

He's such a dear is Alfie Moon,
With big brown eyes like limpid lakes.
A look's enough to make you swoon.
A glance—that's all it takes.

A cuddly bundle when he came
He gave us so much fun.
Before he'd even got a name—
Was loved by everyone.

And as he grew, began to chew
Just everything in sight.
The door, the floor, the chair, my shoe,
And woke us in the night!

But now he's had some training
Our dog behaves indoors.
And even if its raining
We don't mind his muddy paws.

HOME GOAL

I wandered lonely as a fish
That swims without a mate,
When, round the bend, as if a wish
Had suddenly come true
I saw a crowd of football fans
In vivid gold and blue.
And there amongst the heaving throng
I saw, 'midst all the rest,
A foreign body, tall and strong
But—in a purple vest!

How came he there I could not say,
He must be all at sea.
So to spare him further blushes
I took him home for tea.

Serious Business!

I really have to sleep right now.
I just can't stay awake;
I've finished all the heavy work
And eaten too much cake.

Tomorrow I will have a rest,
Perhaps I'll read my book.
The reading club is nearly due
I'd better take a look.

Our reading group meets once a month
For serious reviews;
Then cups of tea and chatter turns
To all the local news!

CODE WORDS

4 must be U
Because 10 is Q.
But if T is 7
Then what is 11?
I just cannot see
A letter for 3!

Somewhere I've gone wrong;
Its taking too long;
I'll try *once* more
Now, what's 24?

THE COMPUTER BUFF

Don't spin just now, the signals weak.
Carry on and its sure to break.
Try Googling it or even Ask;
Creating a web is such a task!
The spider spins—
Her web is strong.
My web's a mess,
Its all gone wrong.
I've pressed all the keys,
And paced the house,
I need a spider not a mouse!

But I carried on determinedly and there's something
now to make me proud.
The total sum of all my work has turned into a '**cloud**'!

MINCING WAYS

When money was always in short supply
They often had to rough it.
Lots of make-do's and tightening of belts,
Yes, they really had to rough it.

The cooking back then would make you wince.
The rooms were cold, the lights were dim,
And they fed on platefuls of mince!
A hundred ways of cooking the stuff;
She tried her best but it sure was tough.
There certainly was an incentive
For the cook to be inventive.
But it took a while to bring a smile,
To extinguish the dinner time wince.

It's a pretty fair bet that ever since
They all hate MINCE!

JINGLE TILLS

(A parody on Jingle Bells!)

Jingle tills, jingle tills,
Jingle all the day.
Oh, my word, just realised
Its almost Christmas Day!
Oh, how they ring, jingle tills,
Busy every day.
Not long now, nearly here,
Its almost Christmas Day!

Dashing through the shops,
Struggling all the way;
Jostling, bumping,—gosh what crowds,
Its almost Christmas day!

Jingle tills, jingle tills,
What more can one say?
How about the meaning of
The first *real* Christmas Day?

DRAMA

Do you see the action?
Can you hear the sound?
Are you participating?
Theatre in the round!

Have you heard the story?
Its an old one, I'll be bound,
With a new interpretation—
Theatre in the round!

Will they catch the villain?
Surely he'll be found.
For him there is no hiding place.
THEATRE IN THE ROUND!

CHAMPAGNE

Champagne is a name
With a claim to fame.
It's expensive and fizzy,
Can make you feel dizzy.
A tad over-rated?
(By some its just hated!)
I like it a lot
But, do you know what?
Its such a palaver
I'd rather have Cava!

THE WEDDING

Tell me, tell me, is this true—
We're standing here to say 'I do'?

I'm not sure how this came to be;
You—in a suit!
Right next to me.

But seeing as how we've got this far
Let's tie the knot and find the bar!

MILLENNIUM

To herald in a new era

Medieval times are past, modern age is here at last,
Incandescence all around!
Light and form and sound abound.
Long thin models, lorries, litter.
Every day more gossip and glitter!
Newly discovered jungles explored; every idol duly
adored.
Nothing, but nothing is left to chance: no-one escapes
the millennium dance.
In order that progress is given a shot changes are made,
whether needed or not.
Untold havoc; progressive ideas, some good, some
bad, and others quite mad!
Millennium wishes, millennium hopes; can anyone
tell our horoscopes?

It's a Funny Old Life

The bottle was empty, not a drop came out!
She didn't know whether to cry or shout.
Her heart was broken.

It truly lay in tatters,
As surely as a window shatters
When hit by a stone
Or a stray golf ball
Or a hail stone fall
Or a meteorite—

"Oh stop! You're tight!"
She muttered to herself.
"You're on the shelf!
Face up to the fact
He won't come back.
He's got a wife—
It's a funny old life."